CONTENTS

POKÉMON™
BATTLE FRONTIER
ANNUAL 2008

Published by Pedigree Books Limited, Beech Hill House, Walnut Gardens, Exeter, Devon EX4 4DH. Published 2007.

Pedigree®

£7.99

MEET THE POKÉMON PALS

ASH

Ash is a renowned and energetic Trainer from Pallet Town. He is brave, caring and determined, but he can sometimes be reckless and stubborn too. He is on a quest to become the greatest Pokémon Master. To achieve this ambition, he travels around with his companions, battling Gym Leaders and entering in competitions.

In battle, Ash is very competitive and he can show great skill. Throughout his adventures in the world of Pokmon, he has matured and improved as a trainer. His focus has remained just as strong, but now he must confront the Frontier Brains. With new Pokémon to discover and his loyal friends by his side, what new adventures lie in store for Ash?

PICKACHU

Pikachu was Ash's first Pokémon. Even though they got off to a rocky start, they're now a terrific team! Pikachu has remained a loyal and true friend. There is a powerful bond between Ash and Pikachu, and there is something unique about this particular Pikachu that sets it apart from others.

Pikachu's name resembles the way Pikachu speaks. Team Rocket never gives up trying to steal Pikachu, but their attempts always seem to end in

BROCK

Brock's dream is to become the greatest Pokémon Breeder, and he has journeyed with Ash on many adventures. He is always well equipped and he loves to help others. He is a hard worker and he is also kind and calm.

Whenever Ash needs a friend or a few wise words of advice, Brock is always there. He is a wonderful cook and he often makes delicious meals for his companions. He just has one weakness – pretty girls! Whenever he sees one, he can't help falling in love …

MEET THE POKÉMON PALS

MAY

May is a sweet, kind-hearted girl and a talented Pokémon Coordinator. She met Ash when she was just starting out as a Pokémon Trainer, and she decided to travel with him so that she could learn from him.

May doesn't know very much about Pokémon, but she is eager to learn, and she prefers to focus on winning ribbons rather than gym badges. Therefore she enters her Pokémon in Contests, where they are judged on the beauty of their attacks rather than their power.

MAX

Max is May's younger brother, and he can't wait to become a Pokémon Trainer. He travels with Ash, May and Brock to pick up al the skills and knowledge he can. When he is old enough to become a Pokémon Trainer, he wants to be way ahead of the game! Max can be a bit of a know-it-all, but he really cares about Pokémon and his sister.

TEAM ROCKET

Team Rocket is the trio who want to steal Pokémon and use them to gain money and power. However, they are never quite as quick or intelligent as Ash and his friends, and they are always getting themselves into trouble! They want to steal Pikachu from Ash, but they haven't succeeded yet.

Jessie is Team Rocket's beautiful, talented superstar – in her own mind, that is!

James ran away from his rich parents to become a poor Team Rocket member!

Meowth is a wise-cracking Pokémon who is always inventing new criminal capers for the trio to try.

Team Rocket call Ash and his friends 'the twerps'. They are masters of disguise … but their plans always seem to end in Team Rocket blasting

COPY COOL

▶▶▶ Check out this picture of Ash playing with Pikachu and Treecko. Use your felt tips or colouring pencils to finish the drawing. Can you match the colours in the small picture?

CROSS WORDS

>>>> Solve the clues and complete the crossword. Time yourself and find out how speedy you are. See how many clues you can solve without checking the answers! (Some letters have been left in to help you.)

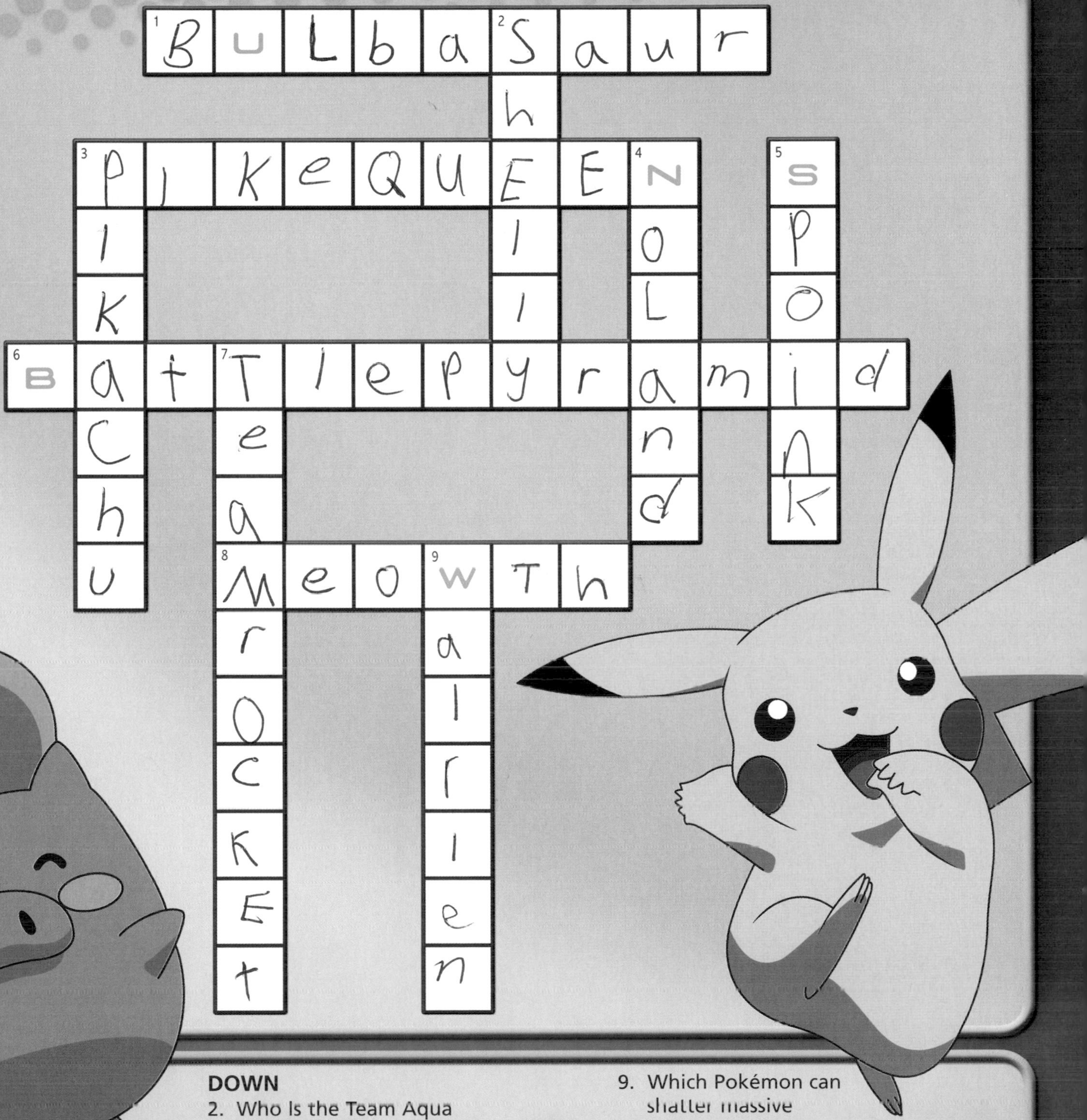

Crossword grid (handwritten answers):

- 1 Across: B U L B A S A U R
- 2 Down: S H E I L L
- 3 Across: P I K E Q U E E N
- 3 Down: P I K A C H U
- 4 Down: N O L L A N D
- 5 Down: S P O I N K
- 6 Across: B A T T L E P Y R A M I D
- 7 Down: T E A M R O C K E T
- 8 Across: M E O W T H
- 9 Down: W A I L E I N

DOWN
2. Who Is the Team Aqua Commander? (6)
3. Anagram: A uk chip. (7)
4. Who is the head of the Battle Factory? (6)
5. Which Pokémon bounces around on its tail to keep its heart pumping? (6)
7. Anagram: Meet at cork. (4,6)

9. Which Pokémon can shatter massive icebergs with its tusks? (7)

ACROSS
1. Which Pokémon is listed as Pokédex number 1? (9)
3. What is Lucy's title? (4,5)
6. Where does Brandon live? (6,7)
8. Which Pokémon is a member of Team Rocket? (6)

11

001 BULBASAUR
TYPE>> Grass/Poison
ABILITY>> Overgrow

002 IVYSAUR
TYPE>> Grass/Poison
ABILITY>> Overgrow

003 VENUSAUR
TYPE>> Grass/Poison
ABILITY>> Overgrow

004 CHARMANDER
TYPE>> Fire
ABILITY>> Blaze

005 CHARMELEON
TYPE>> Fire
ABILITY>> Blaze

006 CHARIZARD
TYPE>> Fire/Flying
ABILITY>> Blaze

007 SQUIRTLE
TYPE>> Water
ABILITY>> Torrent

008 WARTORTLE
TYPE>> Water
ABILITY>> Torrent

009 BLASTOISE
TYPE>> Water
ABILITY>> Torrent

010 CATERPIE
TYPE>> Bug
ABILITY>> Shield Dust

011 METAPOD
TYPE>> Bug
ABILITY>> Shed Skin

012 BUTTERFREE
TYPE>> Bug/Flying
ABILITY>> Compoundeyes

013 WEEDLE
TYPE>> Bug/Poison
ABILITY>> Shield Dust

014 KAKUNA
TYPE>> Bug/Poison
ABILITY>> Shed Skin

015 BEEDRILL
TYPE>> Bug/Poison
ABILITY>> Swarm

016 PIDGEY
TYPE>> Normal/Flying
ABILITY>> Keen Eye

017 PIDGEOTTO
TYPE>> Normal/Flying
ABILITY>> Keen Eye

018 PIDGEOT
TYPE>> Normal/Flying
ABILITY>> Keen Eye

019 RATTATA
TYPE>> Normal
ABILITY>> Run Away/Guts

020 RATICATE
TYPE>> Normal
ABILITY>> Run Away/Guts

021 SPEAROW
TYPE>> Normal/Flying
ABILITY>> Keen Eye

022 FEAROW
TYPE>> Normal/Flying
ABILITY>> Keen Eye

023 EKANS
TYPE>> Poison
ABILITY>> Intimidate/Shed Skin

024 ARBOK
TYPE>> Poison
ABILITY>> Intimidate/Shed Skin

025 PIKACHU	026 RAICHU	027 SANDSHREW	028 SANDSLASH

TYPE>> Electric	TYPE>> Electric	TYPE>> Ground	TYPE>> Ground
ABILITY>> Static	ABILITY>> Static	ABILITY>> Sand Veil	ABILITY>> Sand Veil

029 NIDORAN	030 NIDORINA	031 NIDOQUEEN	032 NIDORAN
TYPE>> Poison	TYPE>> Poison	TYPE>> Poison/Ground	TYPE>> Poison
ABILITY>> Poison Point	ABILITY>> Poison Point	ABILITY>> Poison Point	ABILITY>> Poison Point

033 NIDORINO	034 NIDOKING	035 CLEFAIRY	036 CLEFABLE
TYPE>> Poison	TYPE>> Poison/Ground	TYPE>> Normal	TYPE>> Normal
ABILITY>> Poison Point	ABILITY>> Poison Point	ABILITY>> Cute Charm	ABILITY>> Cute Charm

037 VULPIX	038 NINETALES	039 JIGGLYPUFF	040 WIGGLYTUFF
TYPE>> Fire	TYPE>> Fire	TYPE>> Normal	TYPE>> Normal
ABILITY>> Flash Fire	ABILITY>> Flash Fire	ABILITY>> Cute Charm	ABILITY>> Cute Charm

041 ZUBAT	042 GOLBAT	043 ODDISH	044 GLOOM
TYPE>> Poison/Flying	TYPE>> Poison/Flying	TYPE>> Grass/Poison	TYPE>> Grass/Poison
ABILITY>> Inner Focus	ABILITY>> Inner Focus	ABILITY>> Chlorophyll	ABILITY>> Chlorophyll

045 VILEPLUME	046 PARAS	047 PARASECT	048 VENONAT
TYPE>> Grass/Poison	TYPE>> Bug/Grass	TYPE>> Bug/Grass	TYPE>> Bug/Poison
ABILITY>> Chlorophyll	ABILITY>> Effect Spore	ABILITY>> Effect Spore	ABILITY>> Compoundeyes

049 VENOMOTH	050 DIGLETT	051 DUGTRIO	052 MEOWTH
TYPE>> Bug/Poison	TYPE>> Ground	TYPE>> Ground	TYPE>> Normal
ABILITY>> Shield Dust	ABILITY>> Sand Veil/Arena Trap	ABILITY>> Sand Veil/Arena Trap	ABILITY>> Pickup

053 PERSIAN	054 PSYDUCK	055 GOLDUCK	056 MANKEY
TYPE>> Normal	TYPE>> Water	TYPE>> Water	TYPE>> Fighting
ABILITY>> Limber	ABILITY>> Damp/Cloud Nine	ABILITY>> Damp/Cloud Nine	ABILITY>> Vital Spirit

057 PRIMEAPE	058 GROWLITHE	059 ARCANINE	060 POLIWAG
TYPE>> Fighting	TYPE>> Fire	TYPE>> Fire	TYPE>> Water
ABILITY>> Vital Spirit	ABILITY>> Intimidate/Flash Fire	ABILITY>> Intimidate/Flash Fire	ABILITY>> Water Absorb/Damp

061 POLIWHIRL	062 POLIWRATH	063 ABRA	064 KADABRA
TYPE>> Water	TYPE>> Water/Fighting	TYPE>> Psychic	TYPE>> Psychic
ABILITY>> Water Absorb/Damp	ABILITY>> Water Absorb/Damp	ABILITY>> Synchronize/Inner Focus	ABILITY>> Synchronize/Inner Focus

065 ALAKAZAM	066 MACHOP	067 MACHOKE	068 MACHAMP
TYPE>> Psychic	TYPE>> Fighting	TYPE>> Fighting	TYPE>> Fighting
ABILITY>> Synchronize/Inner Focus	ABILITY>> Guts	ABILITY>> Guts	ABILITY>> Guts

069 BELLSPROUT	070 WEEPINBELL	071 VICTREEBEL	072 TENTACOOL
TYPE>> Grass/Poison	TYPE>> Grass/Poison	TYPE>> Grass/Poison	TYPE>> Water/Poison
ABILITY>> Chlorophyll	ABILITY>> Chlorophyll	ABILITY>> Chlorophyll	ABILITY>> Clear Body/Liquid Ooze

073 TENTACRUEL	074 GEODUDE	075 GRAVELER	076 GOLEM

TYPE>> Water/Poison	TYPE>> Rock/Ground	TYPE>> Rock/Ground	TYPE>> Rock/Ground
ABILITY>> Clear Body/Liquid Ooze	ABILITY>> Rock Head/Sturdy	ABILITY>> Rock Head/Sturdy	ABILITY>> Rock Head/Sturdy

077 PONYTA	078 RAPIDASH	079 SLOWPOKE	080 SLOWBRO
TYPE>> Fire	TYPE>> Fire	TYPE>> Water/Psychic	TYPE>> Water/Psychic
ABILITY>> Run Away/Flash Fire	ABILITY>> Run Away/Flash Fire	ABILITY>> Oblivious/Own Tempo	ABILITY>> Oblivious/Own Tempo

081 MAGNEMITE	082 MAGNETON	083 FARFETCH'D	084 DODUO
TYPE>> Electric/Steel	TYPE>> Electric/Steel	TYPE>> Normal/Flying	TYPE>> Normal/Flying
ABILITY>> Magnet Pull/Sturdy	ABILITY>> Magnet Pull/Sturdy	ABILITY>> Keen Eye/Inner Focus	ABILITY>> Run Away/Early Bird

085 DODRIO	086 SEEL	087 DEWGONG	088 GRIMER
TYPE>> Normal/Flying	TYPE>> Water	TYPE>> Water/Ice	TYPE>> Poison
ABILITY>> Run Away/Early Bird	ABILITY>> Thick Fat	ABILITY>> Thick Fat	ABILITY>> Stench/Sticky Hold

089 MUK	090 SHELLDER	091 CLOYSTER	092 GASTLY
TYPE>> Poison	TYPE>> Water	TYPE>> Water/Ice	TYPE>> Ghost/Poison
ABILITY>> Stench/Sticky Hold	ABILITY>> Shell Armour	ABILITY>> Shell Armour	ABILITY>> Levitate

093 HAUNTER	094 GENGAR	095 ONIX	096 DROWZEE
TYPE>> Ghost/Poison	TYPE>> Ghost/Poison	TYPE>> Rock/Ground	TYPE>> Psychic
ABILITY>> Levitate	ABILITY>> Levitate	ABILITY>> Rock Head/Sturdy	ABILITY>> Insomnia

HIDDEN POKÉMON

▶▶▶ Write the answers to the clues in the grid below to find out which Misterious Pokémon is hiding from Ash and his friends!

1. J a m e s
2. a s h
3. A n a b e l
4. p i k a c h u
5. S p e n c e r
6. m e o w t h
7. M a y

1. Jessie's purple-haired companion.

2. The adventurous young Trainer who dreams of becoming the greatest ever Pokémon Master.

3. The Battle Tower's Salon Maiden.

4. A brave, yellow electric Pokémon.

5. The head of the Battle Palace.

6. The Pokémon member of Team Rocket.

7. Max's older sister.

16

WATER-TYPE WORD SEARCH

There are nine Water-type Pokémon hidden in this grid. Can you spot them all? Tick each one off as you find it.

Blastoise ✓ Feebas ✓ Politoed ✓
Clamperl ✓ Horsea ✓ Wailord ✓
Corphish ✓ Magikarp ✓ Wartortle ✓

Q	Y	R	H	I	F	D	G	S	B	Y	O	H	J	P
L	J	G	F	D	S	R	G	M	F	L	I	A	R	L
Z	E	E	H	K	C	C	E	H	K	R	B	A	Q	S
M	N	L	C	X	A	L	A	D	G	G	K	M	Q	E
H	Y	T	A	B	L	A	S	T	O	I	S	E	R	T
G	G	R	E	K	A	M	E	K	G	H	F	E	D	H
X	R	O	G	H	J	P	Q	A	W	H	N	M	R	Y
M	N	T	V	C	P	E	M	R	F	E	E	B	A	S
H	G	R	L	O	O	R	B	D	E	W	A	S	J	H
L	O	A	U	J	L	L	N	H	T	R	H	F	B	C
B	T	W	S	J	I	K	N	H	V	D	O	E	Z	L
L	L	T	Y	D	T	H	S	I	H	P	R	O	C	W
A	W	A	I	L	O	R	D	G	K	K	S	E	F	X
V	X	W	W	T	E	T	Y	U	I	W	E	L	K	I
L	B	H	U	T	S	D	R	Y	V	X	E	A	I	J

17

SWEET BABY JAMES

Something was very wrong with May's Munchlax. It had a terrible fever! "We'd better get to a Pokémon Centre right away!" said Brock, urgently.

But they weren't anywhere near a Pokémon Centre!

"*Now* what are we gonna do?" cried May.

Suddenly they heard a sweet, calm voice.

"Now what seems to be the trouble, kids?" said an old lady.

"My Munchlax is feeling really sick and I don't know what to do!" said May in a worried voice.

"I'm sure I can help!" said the lady.

The old lady was called Nanny. She and her husband, Pop-Pop, looked after weak and ill Pokémon. They had a sweet little Mime Jr. with them. Mime Jr. can imitate anyone it sees. It can sense people's emotions and erects a barrier to escape when it senses danger.

Not far away, James's
Chimecho was in real pain!
"Meowth, how hard can it be
to read a Pokémon Centre
map?" James snapped.
"Oh 'dis one's *real* easy,
'cause 'dere ain't nuttin' *on*
it!" said Meowth
sarcastically.
"What?" groaned James.
"We *could* use Heal Bell you
know ..." said Jessie.
But Chimecho was too weak
to use its own powers!
"There's *got* to be one!" cried
James, running and
searching. "I won't *stop* until
I find a Pokémon Centre!"
Suddenly he spotted a house.
"Could it be ...?" he asked
quietly. It is!"
He raced inside, calling
"Nanny! Pop-Pop!"
"My!" Nanny exclaimed.
"Well, if it isn't L'il James!"

"L'il?" repeated Jessie and Meowth in amazement.
"I'm so glad to see you!" James said to Nanny and Pop-Pop.
"Nice to see you too!" smiled Pop-Pop.
"And in such good health!" Nanny added.
"Thanks," said James. "I wish I could say the same for Chimecho."
Pop-Pop and Nanny examined Chimecho.
"Yep, somethin's not right," said Pop-Pop eventually.

"Now don't worry, L'il James!" said Nanny.
Pop-Pop suddenly noticed Jessie and Meowth.
"L'il James? Are those two friends of yours?" he asked.
"Jessie's actually my personal secretary, and my personal butler is Meowth," James replied.
"Secretary and butler, eh?" said

James pulled Jessie and Meowth to one side.

"Okay, so what's the deal?" Jessie asked.

"This is one of my summer cottages," said James, sheepishly. "I used to visit my Nanny and Pop-Pop *every* summer when I was small."

James explained that his time with kind Nanny and Pop-Pop had been a wonderful escape from his strict home life.

"Don't you see?" he said. "I just *had* to show them what a complete success I've become!"

"Wow," said Jessie.

"I could see it bein' a bumma' tellin' 'em you're a Team Rocket guy," Meowth added. "Well you can count on *us*!"

"But you're going to owe us both *big time*!" said Jessie.

"Deal!" replied James.

"Somethin' wrong?" asked Nanny, noticing them whispering.

"No way!" Jessie exclaimed. "Nothing beats being executive secretary of the great and powerful James!"

"Bein' manager's a dream come true!" said Meowth.

"That's nice," said Nanny, "but we have a sick child here."

"Nanny, help us!" James begged.

"It looks to me like the problem here is your Chimecho's exhausted!" said Pop-Pop.

"I'm afraid this poor child needs a good long rest," Nanny added.

"Right, Chime?" said James softly.

Just then, Nanny and Pop-Pop's Mime Jr. Pokémon appeared!

"Cutie-pie!" Jessie squealed.

Suddenly they heard a familiar voice.

"Excuse me? I need water for my Pokémon." Ash and his friends were standing in the doorway!

They all stared at each other in shock. Then James ran towards them as fast as he could and pushed them out of the door.

"All right!" said Ash suspiciously. "What are *you* doin' here?"

"You watch your step!" said Brock sternly. "There's a nice old man and woman living here that help injured Pokémon!"

"*Will you* give it a *rest*?" James hissed.

He leaned forward and explained the situation to them. Brock, May, Ash and Max could hardly believe their ears.

"But what are you twerps doing here?" asked James.

"My Munchlax was feeling really sick and your Nanny and Pop-Pop offered to help us!" said May.

"*Why* am I not surprised?" James said with a chuckle.

"So ... since we've all ended up here, what do you say we call a truce?"

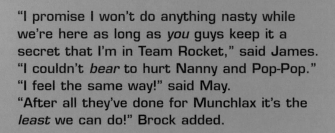

"I promise I won't do anything nasty while we're here as long as *you* guys keep it a secret that I'm in Team Rocket," said James. "I couldn't *bear* to hurt Nanny and Pop-Pop."
"I feel the same way!" said May.
"After all they've done for Munchlax it's the *least* we can do!" Brock added.

Nanny and Pop-Pop opened the door and peered out.
"Are all these young people your friends too?" asked Pop-Pop.
"Of course!" James declared. "*Best* friends!"
"Wonder where your secretary and manager went off to," said Pop-Pop.

James found Jessie and Meowth by the fridge, cramming food into their mouths as fast as they could. "I should've known!" James scowled. "Where are your *manners*? That is *not* your food!"

"So what else are you supposed to do when you're hungry?" asked Jessie innocently.

"Stop!" said James, annoyed. "You two promised me you'd be good!"

"Now what's all the ruckus?" asked Pop-Pop, appearing behind James.

"Why don't you go and show everyone the Pokémon House?" Nanny said to James.

The Pokémon House was a fascinating place, full of interesting and unusual Pokémon!

"It's just like I remember!" said James in excitement.

"When James was a little boy he just loved this place to pieces!" said Nanny.

"We've got all *kinds* of Pokémon in here!" said Pop-Pop. "Spinarak, Aipom ... and, of course, the Woopers!"

"Wow!" cried Max in excitement. "I've never seen Woopers like that!"

"I'm impressed," said Jessie. An Oddish suddenly sped past.

"Wow, the Oddish can *hustle*!" said Jessie.

"Primo Pokémon for poachin'!" said Meowth.

They slipped away and grabbed the Oddish, but James saw them.

"Where did you get *that*?" asked James in shock. James freed the little Pokémon.

"You promised!" he hissed furiously. "No funny stuff!"

That night, James sat by Chimecho's sick bed. Munchlax was there too, and Mime Jr. was watching. May came to see Munchlax.

"I know everything's going to be just fine," said James kindly.

"I sure hope you're right," said May.

"Besides, I'll stay here tonight and keep an eye on things," James added.

"How's your Chimecho doing?" May asked.

"A little better, I think," James replied. "It's my fault. I shouldn't have brought Chimecho this far. But don't worry about a thing! You just get yourself some sleep!"

"I will," said May. "Thank you! Sleep well, Munchlax."

But not far away, trouble was brewing ...

Soon, James was fast asleep by the sick beds, dreaming of Pokémon.
"Sleep, my l'il James...dream on," Jessie whispered, leaning over him.
"While you get some shut-eye we'll get *busy*!" giggled Meowth.
"First we bag Mime Jr. and Munchlax too," said Jessie, putting the Pokémon into her bag.
"'Den 'da whole Pokémon House crew!" said Meowth.

Ash heard something and woke up with a jump. He saw that someone was in the Pokémon House.
"Team Rocket!" yelled Ash, furiously. Ash woke his friends and they all rushed to the Pokémon House.
"Where do you think you're going with those Pokémon?" shouted May.

James was awoken by all the noise. He saw the lights in the Pokémon House and hurried over. "You promised to behave your bad selves!" he yelled.
"Asking *us* to behave is like asking a baby not to cry!" said Jessie angrily.
"An' we're babies all right!" shouted Meowth.
"Seviper, let's *go*!" yelled Jessie, preparing for battle.
"Phanpy, I choose *you*!" Ash cried.
"Seviper, Poison Tail!" Jessie ordered.
"Rollout, Phanpy – *now*!" yelled Ash.

Seviper and Phanpy fought, but Phanpy's attack knocked Seviper out!
"Cacnea, let's go!" James cried, throwing his Pokéball.
He told Cacnea to battle Seviper!
"You turncoat!" said Jessie angrily.
"What're you doin' sidin' wit' 'da twoips?" Meowth hissed.
"I'm siding with Nanny and Pop-Pop!" James declared. "Cacnea, use Sandstorm!"

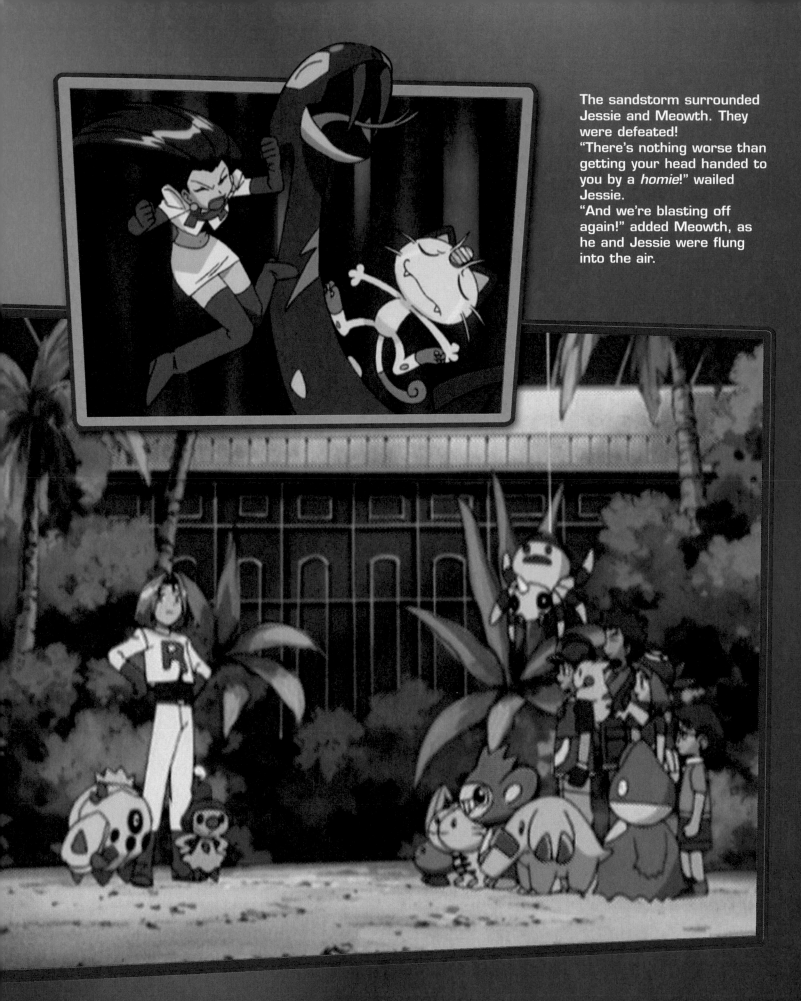

The sandstorm surrounded Jessie and Meowth. They were defeated!
"There's nothing worse than getting your head handed to you by a *homie*!" wailed Jessie.
"And we're blasting off again!" added Meowth, as he and Jessie were flung into the air.

Just then, Nanny and Pop-Pop came running.
"Now, what're you doing up at all hours of the night?" asked Pop-Pop.
"I guess I was reliving my childhood and playing with all the Pokémon!" said James.
"It does a heart good to see all these young people here!" said Nanny.

Early next day, Ash and his friends were ready to leave.
"Munchlax has got that famous appetite back and feels *great*, thanks to you!" May told Nanny and Pop-Pop.
"Thanks!" said Ash. "Take care!"
The friends waved goodbye.
Jessie and Meowth were waiting in the Team Rocket balloon for James. But Chimecho was still poorly.

"Don't worry," said Nanny quietly. "I think Chimecho just needs more rest."
Chimecho lifted its head, as if to say, "I'm okay! You go on ahead, James."
"Chime!" said James, trying to hold back his tears as he thought of all the good times they had spent together.

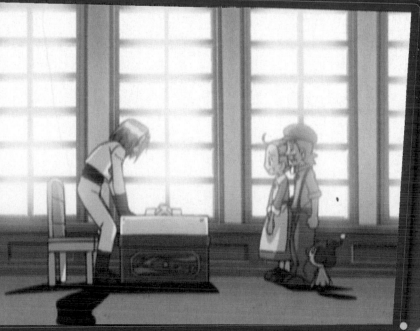

"Take care of Chime," James urged Nanny and Pop-Pop.

"Just like one of our babies," Nanny promised.

James pulled out Chimecho's Poké Ball and an empty one fell to the floor. Mime Jr. jumped into it!

"Mime Jr.?" said James, surprised. "What just happened?"

"It's lookin' to me like you just found yourself a good buddy in Mime Jr.!" said Pop-Pop.

"Mime Jr. has an amazin' way of pickin' up on peoples' emotions, and could tell you were feelin' kinda' lonely," said Nanny. "Why don't you take along your new friend?"

James had found a brand-new Pokémon friend!

"Before we go, I've got something to tell you both," said James. He took a deep breath and finally plucked up the courage to tell them the truth about himself!

"I still can't believe that our L'il James got all mixed up with that Team Rocket," said Pop-Pop, when James had gone. They watched the balloon fly into the distance. "Me neither," said Nanny, "but he's still the same sweetheart he was when he was just a little boy." She smiled at Pop-Pop. "As long as he's happy, then I am too," she said. "Right!" said Pop-Pop.

MATCHING POKÉMON

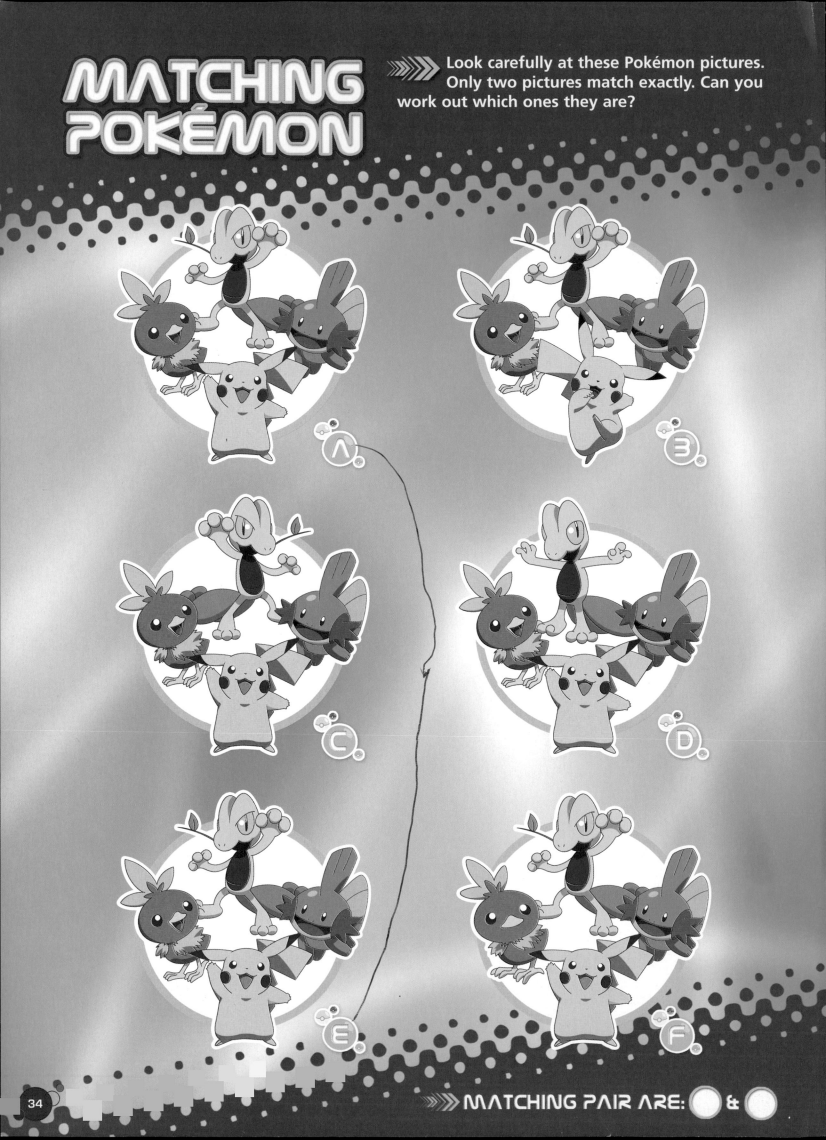

>>> Look carefully at these Pokémon pictures. Only two pictures match exactly. Can you work out which ones they are?

>>> MATCHING PAIR ARE: ◯ & ◯

A.

B.

C.

D.

E.

F.

WHICH WAY MAZE

May has been separated from her friends. She has to get through the maze to catch up with Ash, but Team Rocket is trying to stop her! Can you show her the way through the maze to safety?

097 HYPNO	098 KRABBY	099 KINGLER	100 VOLTORB
TYPE>> Psychic	TYPE>> Water	TYPE>> Water	TYPE>> Electric
ABILITY>> Insomnia	ABILITY>> Hyper Cutter/Shell Armour	ABILITY>> Hyper Cutter/Shell Armour	ABILITY>> Soundproof/Static

101 ELECTRODE	102 EXEGGCUTE	103 EXEGGUTOR	104 CUBONE
TYPE>> Electric	TYPE>> Grass/Psychic	TYPE>> Grass/Psychic	TYPE>> Ground
ABILITY>> Soundproof/Static	ABILITY>> Chlorophyll	ABILITY>> Chlorophyll	ABILITY>> Rock Head/Lightningrod

105 MAROWAK	106 HITMONLEE	107 HITMONCHAN	108 LICKITUNG
TYPE>> Ground	TYPE>> Fighting	TYPE>> Fighting	TYPE>> Normal
ABILITY>> Rock Head/Lightningrod	ABILITY>> Limber	ABILITY>> Keen Eye	ABILITY>> Own Tempo/Oblivious

109 KOFFING	110 WEEZING	111 RHYHORN	112 RHYDON
TYPE>> Poison	TYPE>> Poison	TYPE>> Ground/Rock	TYPE>> Ground/Rock
ABILITY>> Levitate	ABILITY>> Levitate	ABILITY>> Lightning Rod/Rock Head	ABILITY>> Lightning Rod/Rock Head

113 CHANSEY	114 TANGELA	115 KANGASKHAN	116 HORSEA
TYPE>> Normal	TYPE>> Grass	TYPE>> Normal	TYPE>> Water
ABILITY>> Natural Cure/Serene Grace	ABILITY>> Chlorophyll	ABILITY>> Early Bird	ABILITY>> Swift Swim

117 SEADRA	118 GOLDEEN	119 SEAKING	120 STARYU
TYPE>> Water	TYPE>> Water	TYPE>> Water	TYPE>> Water
ABILITY>> Poison Point	ABILITY>> Swift Swim/Water Veil	ABILITY>> Swift Swim/Water Veil	ABILITY>> Illuminate/Natural Cure

121 STARMIE	122 MR. MIME	123 SCYTHER	124 JYNX
TYPE>> Water/Psychic	TYPE>> Psychic	TYPE>> Bug/Flying	TYPE>> Ice/Psychic
ABILITY>> Illuminate/Natural Cure	ABILITY>> Soundproof	ABILITY>> Swarm	ABILITY>> Oblivious

125 ELECTABUZZ	126 MAGMAR	127 PINSIR	128 TAUROS
TYPE>> Electric	TYPE>> Fire	TYPE>> Bug	TYPE>> Normal
ABILITY>> Static	ABILITY>> Flame Body	ABILITY>> Hyper Cutter	ABILITY>> Intimidate

129 MAGIKARP	130 GYARADOS	131 LAPRAS	132 DITTO
TYPE>> Water	TYPE>> Water/Flying	TYPE>> Water/Ice	TYPE>> Normal
ABILITY>> Swift Swim	ABILITY>> Intimidate	ABILITY>> Water Absorb/Shell Armour	ABILITY>> Limber

133 EEVEE	134 VAPOREON	135 JOLTEON	136 FLAREON
TYPE>> Normal	TYPE>> Water	TYPE>> Electic	TYPE>> Fire
ABILITY>> Run Away	ABILITY>> Water Absorb	ABILITY>> Volt Absorb	ABILITY>> Flash Fire

137 PORYGON	138 OMANYTE	139 OMASTAR	140 KABUTO
TYPE>> Normal	TYPE>> Rock/Water	TYPE>> Rock/Water	TYPE>> Rock/Water
ABILITY>> Trace	ABILITY>> Swift Swim/Shell Armour	ABILITY>> Swift Swim/Shell Armour	ABILITY>> Swift Swim/Battle Armour

141 KABUTOPS	142 AERODACTYL	143 SNORLAX	144 ARTICUNO
TYPE>> Rock/Water	TYPE>> Rock/Flying	TYPE>> Normal	TYPE>> Ice/Flying
ABILITY>> Swift swim/Battle Armour	ABILITY>> Rock Head/Pressure	ABILITY>> Immunity/Thick Fat	ABILITY>> Pressure

145 ZAPDOS	146 MOLTRES	147 DRATINI	148 DRAGONAIR
TYPE>> Electric/Flying	TYPE>> Fire/Flying	TYPE>> Dragon	TYPE>> Dragon
ABILITY>> Pressure	ABILITY>> Pressure	ABILITY>> Shed Skin	ABILITY>> Shed Skin

149 DRAGONITE	150 MEWTWO	151 MEW	152 CHIKORITA
TYPE>> Dragon/Flying	TYPE>> Psychic	TYPE>> Psychic	TYPE>> Grass
ABILITY>> Inner Focus	ABILITY>> Pressure	ABILITY>> Synchronize	ABILITY>> Overgrow

153 BAYLEEF	154 MEGANIUM	155 CYNDAQUIL	156 QUILAVA
TYPE>> Grass	TYPE>> Grass	TYPE>> Fire	TYPE>> Fire
ABILITY>> Overgrow	ABILITY>> Overgrow	ABILITY>> Blaze	ABILITY>> Blaze

157 TYPHLOSION	158 TOTODILE	159 CROCONAW	160 FERALIGATR
TYPE>> Fire	TYPE>> Water	TYPE>> Water	TYPE>> Water
ABILITY>> Blaze	ABILITY>> Torrent	ABILITY>> Torrent	ABILITY>> Torrent

161 SENTRET	162 FURRET	163 HOOTHOOT	164 NOCTOWL
TYPE>> Normal	TYPE>> Normal	TYPE>> Normal/Flying	TYPE>> Normal/Flying
ABILITY>> Run Away/Keen Eye	ABILITY>> Run Away/Keen Eye	ABILITY>> Insomina/Keen Eye	ABILITY>> Insomina/Keen Eye

165 LEDYBA	166 LEDIAN	167 SPINARAK	168 ARIADOS
TYPE>> Bug/Flying	TYPE>> Bug/Flying	TYPE>> Bug/Poison	TYPE>> Bug/Poison
ABILITY>> Swarm/Early Bird	ABILITY>> Swarm/Early Bird	ABILITY>> Swarm/Insomnia	ABILITY>> Swarm/Insomnia

169 CROBAT	170 CHINCHOU	171 LANTURN	172 PICHU
TYPE>> Poison/Flying	TYPE>> Water/Electric	TYPE>> Water/Electric	TYPE>> Electric
ABILITY>> Inner Focus	ABILITY>> Volt Absorb/Illuminate	ABILITY>> Volt Absorb/Illuminate	ABILITY>> Static

173 CLEFFA	174 IGGLYBUFF	175 TOGEPI	176 TOGETIC
TYPE>> Normal	TYPE>> Normal	TYPE>> Normal	TYPE>> Normal/Flying
ABILITY>> Cute Charm	ABILITY>> Cute Charm	ABILITY>> Hustle/Serene Grace	ABILITY>> Hustle/Serene Grace

177 NATU	178 XATU	179 MAREEP	180 FLAAFFY
TYPE>> Psychic/Flying	TYPE>> Psychic/Flying	TYPE>> Electric	TYPE>> Electric
ABILITY>> Synchronize/Early Bird	ABILITY>> Synchronize/Early Bird	ABILITY>> Static	ABILITY>> Static

181 AMPHAROS	182 BELLOSSOM	183 MARILL	184 AZUMARILL
TYPE>> Electric	TYPE>> Grass	TYPE>> Water	TYPE>> Water
ABILITY>> Static	ABILITY>> Chlorophyll	ABILITY>> Thick Fat/Huge Power	ABILITY>> Thick Fat/Huge Power

185 SUDOWOODO	186 POLITOED	187 HOPPIP	188 SKIPLOOM
TYPE>> Rock	TYPE>> Water	TYPE>> Grass/Flying	TYPE>> Grass/Flying
ABILITY>> Sturdy/Rock Head	ABILITY>> Water Absorb/Damp	ABILITY>> Chlorophyll	ABILITY>> Chlorophyll

189 JUMPLUFF	190 AIPOM	191 SUNKERN	192 SUNFLORA
TYPE>> Grass/Flying	TYPE>> Normal	TYPE>> Grass	TYPE>> Grass
ABILITY>> Chlorophyll	ABILITY>> Run Away/Pickup	ABILITY>> Chlorophyll	ABILITY>> Chlorophyll

PICTURE PERFECT

>>> Check out these three awesome Pokémon! Choose your favourite and then copy it into the large grid. If you like all three Pokémon, copy the grid onto some extra sheets of paper. Then colour your Pokémon in. Make sure you stay inside the lines!

POKÉ JUGGLING BAGS

>>> A good Pokémon Trainer needs to have quick reflexes and awesome co-ordination. Juggling is a great way to practise these skills. Follow these simple instructions to make your own Poké Juggling Bags!

>>> YOU WILL NEED:

- A piece of red fabric, 12cm x 12cm
- A piece of white fabric, 12cm x 12cm
- A needle and thread
- Dried peas
- A grown-up to help you.

>>> INSTRUCTIONS:

1. Put the two pieces of fabric together so that the sides that will be on the inside are facing outwards.

2. Ask a grown-up to help you stitch all around the outside of the bag. Do not completely finish the stitching - leave a 3cm gap.

3. Turn the bag inside out by pushing it through the hole. The stitching should now be hidden on the inside.

4. Fill the bag with dried peas. Then ask a grown-up to help you stitch up the little hole.

When you have made several Poké Bags, give some to your friends. You can use them as part of your Pokémon games or even learn how to juggle!

TIP:

You can make pyramid-shaped Poké Juggling Bags by cutting the fabric into triangle shapes first!

Ash and his friends were heading towards Fennel Valley, the current location of the travelling Battle Pyramid. Suddenly, Pikachu spotted a new Pokémon, sitting in a tree.

"Pikachu!" said the new Pokémon, sounding exactly like Pikachu.
Ash was amazed. This wasn't a Pikachu!
"Wh – what's that?" he asked.
"It – looks like a Chatot," said Brock.
"Yeah!" said Max in excitement. "It *is* a Chatot – I'm sure of it!"
"It *is* a Chatot! It *is* a Chatot!" mimicked the Chatot.
"Wow, that's funny!" smiled Max.
"Wow that's funny!" repeated the Chatot.
"It repeats whatever you say!" said May, amazed.
Suddenly they heard a voice calling, "There you are!"

STRATEGY TOMORROW, COMEDY TONIGHT

A girl appeared, running at top speed.

"Would you all give me a hand and please grab my Chatot for me?" she asked.

"Grab my Chatot for me!" repeated the Chatot. "Grab my Chatot for me!"

Ash and his friends tried to help, but Chatot did not want to be caught! It flew away from them.

"Come on, Chatot," the girl pleaded. "Don't do this!"

The Chatot landed on a tree stump and Ash threw himself towards it.

"Gotcha!" cried Ash as he grabbed the Pokémon.

"Thank you!" panted the girl, who was out of breath. "My name's Ada, and this is Chatot!"

Ash and his friends introduced themselves.

May checked her Pokédex for information about the Chatot. "Chatot, the Music Pokémon," said the Pokédex. "It copies whatever sounds it hears and arranges them into its own melody."

"So, no matter what they hear someone sayin', they say it *too*!" said Max.

"And they can even memorise complete phrases!" Ada told them.

"Memorise complete phrases!" said Chatot.

"It *is* fun, but it can *also* be – annoying," said Ada.

"Can *also* be – annoying," said Chatot.

"I mean *you*, not *me*!" said Ada.

"*You* not *me*!" said Chatot.

The friends couldn't help but laugh!

"I'm thinking of doing comedy with Chatot," said Ada. "A routine – like Pokémon comedians!"

"You mean stand-up comedy?" asked Max.

"All the big cities in the Johto Region are going to be holding a Comedy Grand Prix!" said Ada. "And it's *always* been my dream to become a famous comedian! The grand prize is a guest spot on a big late night *talk show*!"

"Wow!" said May. "That sounds exciting!"

"We call ourselves the 'Seaside Chat-a-lots'," said Ada.

"So let's see what you've *got*!" said Max.

The others encouraged Ada and she went into her routine.

"Thanks for coming, everybody!" she began. "We're the Seaside Chat-a-lots!"

"Seaside Chat-a-lots!" said Chatot.

"This is my buddy Chatot!" said Ada.

"This is my buddy Chatot!" Chatot mimicked.

"I'm talkin' to you!" said Ada as if she were cross.

"I'm talkin' to you!" said Chatot.

"I'm not a ventriloquist but *you're* a real dummy!" said Ada.

"No, *you're* the real *dummy, Ada*!" said Chatot.

"Look, if I need a writer, I'll *ask*!" said Ada.

Ash, May, Max and Brock laughed and laughed!

"Okay! Now! Chatot's going to do a rap!" said Ada.

"Chatot's gonna do a rap!" said Chatot. "Pika Pikachu, Quick Attack!"

"Pika Quick Attack!" said Ada.

"Pikachu Thunderbolt, whoa!" said Chatot.

"Thunderbolt, let's *go*!" cried Ada.

Ash and his friends were impressed! They clapped loudly.

"Ada, you're *good*!" Ash said, really impressed.

"There's just one problem," said Ada. "As soon as we try and hit the road to fine-tune our act ..."
Ada explained that Chatot always flew away when she tried to set off on a journey.
"And even though Chatot *always* comes back to me at night, the next day it's off once again!" said Ada to her new friends.
"I wonder where Chatot's going," said May.
"Okay! Lunchtime!" said Chatot.
"Chatot's *always* saying weird stuff like that," said Ada.

Not far away, Team Rocket had seen everything. They decided to try to steal the Chatot!

Jessie and James disguised themselves as travelling sales people and approached Ash and his friends.

"Have *we got a Surprise Bag* for you!" they said together.

"We're selling Surprise Bags, like *any* honest salesman!" said James.

"What are Surprise Bags?" asked Max.

"Duh! Bags with a *surprise* in them!" said James.

Ada was interested and bought two.

"I can use them in my Pokémon stand up routine!" she said.

"You'll get a *laugh* all right!" said Jessie and James. "Always a pleasure taking other people's money! Lots of *luck*, suckas!"

They ran away ... and then the Surprise Bags exploded! They were smoke bombs!

"What's happening?" cried Ada.

"Team Rocket!" gasped May and Max.

In the confusion, Team Rocket grabbed Chatot and put it in a cage.

"Come back!" Ash demanded.

"Give me my Chatot!" Ada cried.

"Sorry, no can do," sang out Jessie as they flew away in their balloon.

"Sorry, no can do," Chatot repeated.

"Swellow! Let's *go*!" yelled Ash. "Quick! Use Aerial Ace!"

Swellow attacked and hit the balloon. Chatot fell out and the cage burst open. Chatot was free!

"Chatot *overboard*!" Jessie yelled.

"Let's go, Aipom!" cried Ash. "Swift!"

Aipom attacked, sending Team Rocket flying!

"*Us* overboard!" they screamed. "We're blasting off again!"

"Are you all right?" Ada asked, hugging Chatot.
"Are you all right?" Chatot said.
"Come on, I *mean* it!" Ada insisted.
"Come on, I *mean* it!" Chatot said.
"Okay kids, lights out!"
Ash and his friends looked at Chatot in surprise.
"There's some more of that weird stuff again," said Ada, worried.

"Does Chatot say a *lot* of weird stuff?" Max asked later, over lunch.
"*Lots* of things!" said Ada.
Suddenly, Chatot burst out of its Pokéball and flew away!
"Chatot, *please* come back!" Ada called.
The kids ran after Chatot.
"Come on – you know I can't do the Seaside Chat-a-lots *without* you!" Ada called.
"Can't do without you!" said Chatot.
"Time to check your temperature!"

"What's *that* all about?"
panted May as they ran.
"I hate shots!" cried Chatot.
"That's *completely* weird!" said
Max, puffing.
They ran and ran, but it was
no good. Chatot got away.

"All that stuff it said – maybe
they're *clues*!" Max suggested.
"Let's think of everything
Chatot said," Brock suggested.
"Wasn't the first thing 'It's
lunchtime'?" said May.
"You're right!" said Max. "Then
'Lights out'."
"'Check your temperature',"
said Ada, remembering.
"And 'I hate shots'," said Ash.
"One place comes to mind,"
said Brock.
"It's a hospital!" Max stated.
"Ada, is there a hospital near
here somewhere?" Ash asked.
"It's up on top of the hill!"
said Ada.

In the hospital, Chatot was playing with all the poorly children.
"It's so great to see you!" cried a little girl called Corinna.
"What a nice surprise!" said the nurse.
"I hate shots!" Chatot squawked.
"Oh Chatot, you're just the funniest little thing!" laughed Corinna.
The friends arrived as Chatot was repeating what Corinna had said.
"I'd know *that* voice *anywhere*," said Ada.
"Hi, may I help you?" asked the nurse, leaning out of the window

In the hospital office, Ada explained to the nurse and the hospital chief about how Chatot had been running away.

"A few weeks ago Chatot appeared!" said the nurse. "And you just can't *believe* how much happier the children are now!" said the hospital chief.

"You have *been* busy, haven't you?" said Ada to Chatot. "Cheering up sick kids – *that'll* keep you busy!" said May.

"Chatot's a real hero, *too*!" said Ada.

"Chatot's a real hero!" said Chatot.

"It's great that Chatot's made some new friends," said Ada. "But Chatot and I are actually a comedy team! We're planning on going off on a journey so we can win the Comedy Grand Prix."

"That means Chatot won't be able to come and visit us any more!" said Corinna.
But if they're a comedy team then they have to be *together*, don't they, dear?" said the nurse.
"No!" Corinna yelled. "I don't *care* about that!"
She ran out of the room.
"I have an idea!" said the hospital chief. "Why not do your routine for the children – as practice?"
"Of *course*!" said Ada. "I'd love to!"
"Since we've all got our Pokémon here, maybe we could get in on the act?" said Ash.
"I *know* Corinna would feel a *lot* better if you could do this one thing for her," said the hospital chief.

The friends put on a special Pokémon show – just for the children!
At first, the show was a great success. Brock sang, Ash demonstrated some Pokémon powers and Ada did a hilarious rap with Chatot.

But suddenly Surprise Bags hit the stage, spreading smoke everywhere! The children started to scream.
"Kids, what's *wrong*?" asked May.
"Prepare for trouble!" said a familiar voice.
"Everything's *right*!"
It was Team Rocket!
"We'rc here for one *'ting* – 'dat Chatot!" Meowth hissed. "Show's *ova'*!"
"You're not goin' *anywhere*!" Ash yelled.
"Dustox, prove the Twerp *wrong*!" cried Jessie.
"Sceptile, I choose you!" Ash shouted.
"Dustox, use Tackle *now*!" Jessie ordered.
"Dodge it, Sceptile!" Ash instructed, and Sceptile avoided the attack.

"Poison Sting, let's *go*!" Jessie bellowed.

"Quick Attack, Sceptile!" yelled Ash. Dustox flew backwards! Sceptile and Dustox fought as everyone watched.

"Awesome!" said Corinna. "This is a *real* Pokémon battle!"

"Sceptile, use Bullet Seed!" Ash instructed.

"Use Peck, Chatot!" Ada cried. Meowth got pecked!

"'Dat's a sharp *beak* you got!" Meowth wailed.

"'Dat's a sharp beak you got!" Chatot repeated.

"I don't talk like '*dat*!" Meowth screamed in fury.

"Yes you *do*!" Chatot replied as the children laughed.

"You can *keep* your talking tape recorder!" Jessie yelled as Team Rocket took off in their balloon.

"Sceptile, use Leaf Blade!" Ash cried. Sceptile's attack sent the balloon spinning out of control!

"We're blasting off *again*!" screamed Team Rocket as they shot into the air.

"That was crazy, but fun!" said Ash.
Corinna gave Ada some cookies or Chatot.
"While you're gettin' ready for the Grand Prix, Chatot'll remember us!" she said. "I just *know* you're gonna win the first prize!"
"Thank you!" Ada said.

Soon they were standing at the crossroads. It was time to say goodbye.
"Okay!" said Ada. "Good luck with the Battle Frontier, Ash!"
"And good luck with the Comedy Grand Prix!" Ash replied.
The friends said goodbye to Ada and Chatot, and continued on their journey towards the Battle Pyramid!

193 YANMA	194 WOOPER	195 QUAGSIRE	196 ESPEON
TYPE>> Bug/Flying	TYPE>> Water/Ground	TYPE>> Water/Ground	TYPE>> Psychic
ABILITY>> Speed Boost/Compoundeyes	ABILITY>> Damp/Water Absorb	ABILITY>> Damp/Water Absorb	ABILITY>> Synchronize

197 UMBREON	198 MURKROW	199 SLOWKING	200 MISDREAVUS
TYPE>> Dark	TYPE>> Dark/Flying	TYPE>> Water/Psychic	TYPE>> Ghost
ABILITY>> Synchronize	ABILITY>> Insomnia	ABILITY>> Oblivious/Own Tempo	ABILITY>> Levitate

201 UNOWN	202 WOBBUFFET	203 GIRAFARIG	204 PINECO
TYPE>> Psychic	TYPE>> Psychic	TYPE>> Normal/Psychic	TYPE>> Bug
ABILITY>> Levitate	ABILITY>> Shadow Tag	ABILITY>> Inner Focus/Early Bird	ABILITY>> Sturdy

205 FORRETRESS	206 DUNSPARCE	207 GLIGAR	208 STEELIX
TYPE>> Bug/Steel	TYPE>> Normal	TYPE>> Gound/Flying	TYPE>> Steel/Ground
ABILITY>> Sturdy	ABILITY>> Serene Grace/Run Away	ABILITY>> Hyper Cutter/Sand Veil	ABILITY>> Rock Head/Sturdy

209 SNUBBULL	210 GRANBULL	211 QWILFISH	212 SCIZOR
TYPE>> Normal	TYPE>> Normal	TYPE>> Water/Poison	TYPE>> Bug/Steel
ABILITY>> Intimidate/Run Away	ABILITY>> Intimidate	ABILITY>> Poison Point/Swift Swim	ABILITY>> Swarm

213 SHUCKLE	214 HERACROSS	215 SNEASEL	216 TEDDIURSA
TYPE>> Bug/Rock	TYPE>> Bug/Fighting	TYPE>> Dark Ice	TYPE>> Normal
ABILITY>> Sturdy	ABILITY>> Swarm/Guts	ABILITY>> Inner Focus/Keen Eye	ABILITY>> Pickup

217 URSARING	**218** SLUGMA	**219** MAGCARGO	**220** SWINUB
TYPE>> Normal	TYPE>> Fire	TYPE>> Fire/Rock	TYPE>> Ice/Ground
ABILITY>> Guts	ABILITY>> Magma Armour/Flame Body	ABILITY>> Magma Armour/Flame Body	ABILITY>> Oblivious
221 PILOSWINE	**222** CORSOLA	**223** REMORAID	**224** OCTILLERY
TYPE>> Ice/Ground	TYPE>> Water/Rock	TYPE>> Water	TYPE>> Water
ABILITY>> Oblivious	ABILITY>> Hustle/Natural Cure	ABILITY>> Hustle	ABILITY>> Suction Cups
225 DELIBIRD	**226** MANTINE	**227** SKARMORY	**228** HOUNDOUR
TYPE>> Ice/Flying	TYPE>> Water/Flying	TYPE>> Steel/Flying	TYPE>> Dark/Fire
ABILITY>> Vital Spirit/Hustle	ABILITY>> Swift Swim/Water Absorb	ABILITY>> Keen Eye/Sturdy	ABILITY>> Early Bird/Flash Fire
229 HOUNDOOM	**230** KINGDRA	**231** PHANPY	**232** DONPHAN
TYPE>> Dark/Fire	TYPE>> Water/Dragon	TYPE>> Ground	TYPE>> Ground
ABILITY>> Early Bird/Flash Fire	ABILITY>> Swift Swim	ABILITY>> Pickup	ABILITY>> Sturdy
233 PORYGON2	**234** STANTLER	**235** SMEARGLE	**236** TYROGUE
TYPE>> Normal	TYPE>> Normal	TYPE>> Normal	TYPE>> Fighting
ABILITY>> Trace	ABILITY>> Intimidate	ABILITY>> Own Tempo	ABILITY>> Guts
237 HITMONTOP	**238** SMOOCHUM	**239** ELEKID	**240** MAGBY
TYPE>> Fighting	TYPE>> Ice/Psychic	TYPE>> Electric	TYPE>> Fire
ABILITY>> Intimidate	ABILITY>> Oblivious	ABILITY>> Static	ABILITY>> Flame Body

241 MILTANK	242 BLISSEY	243 RAIKOU	244 ENTEI
TYPE>> Normal	TYPE>> Normal	TYPE>> Electric	TYPE>> Fire
ABILITY>> Thick Fat	ABILITY>> Natural Cure/Serene Grace	ABILITY>> Pressure	ABILITY>> Pressure

245 SUICUNE	246 LARVITAR	247 PUPITAR	248 TYRANITAR
TYPE>> Water	TYPE>> Rock/Ground	TYPE>> Rock/Gound	TYPE>> Dark/Rock
ABILITY>> Pressure	ABILITY>> Guts	ABILITY>> Shed Skin	ABILITY>> Sand Stream

249 LUGIA	250 HO-OH	251 CELEBI	252 TREECKO
TYPE>> Psychic/Flying	TYPE>> Fire/Flying	TYPE>> Grass/Psychic	TYPE>> Grass
ABILITY>> Pressure	ABILITY>> Pressure	ABILITY>> Natural Cure	ABILITY>> Overgrow

253 GROVYLE	254 SCEPTILE	255 TORCHIC	256 COMBUSKEN
TYPE>> Grass	TYPE>> Grass	TYPE>> Fire	TYPE>> Fire/Fighting
ABILITY>> Overgrow	ABILITY>> Overgrow	ABILITY>> Blaze	ABILITY>> Blaze

257 BLAZIKEN	258 MUDKIP	259 MARSHTOMP	260 SWAMPERT
TYPE>> Fire/Fighting	TYPE>> Water	TYPE>> Water/Ground	TYPE>> Water/Ground
ABILITY>> Blaze	ABILITY>> Torrent	ABILITY>> Torrent	ABILITY>> Torrent

261 POOCHYENA	262 MIGHTYENA	263 ZIGZAGOON	264 LINOONE
TYPE>> Dark	TYPE>> Dark	TYPE>> Normal	TYPE>> Normal
ABILITY>> Run Away	ABILITY>> Intimidate	ABILITY>> Pickup	ABILITY>> Pickup

265 WURMPLE	266 SILCOON	267 BEAUTIFLY	268 CASCOON
TYPE>> Bug	TYPE>> Bug	TYPE>> Bug/Flying	TYPE>> Bug
ABILITY>> Shield Dust	ABILITY>> Shed Skin	ABILITY>> Swarm	ABILITY>> Shed Skin

269 DUSTOX	270 LOTAD	271 LOMBRE	272 LUDICOLO
TYPE>> Bug/Poison	TYPE>> Water/Grass	TYPE>> Water/Grass	TYPE>> Water/Grass
ABILITY>> Shield Dust	ABILITY>> Swift Swim/Rain Dish	ABILITY>> Swift Swim/Rain Dish	ABILITY>> Swift Swim/Rain Dish

273 SEEDOT	274 NUZLEAF	275 SHIFTRY	276 TAILLOW
TYPE>> Grass	TYPE>> Grass/Dark	TYPE>> Grass/Dark	TYPE>> Normal/Flying
ABILITY>> Chlorophyll/Early Bird	ABILITY>> Chlorophyll/Early Bird	ABILITY>> Chlorophyll/Early Bird	ABILITY>> Guts

277 SWELLOW	278 WINGULL	279 PELIPPER	280 RALTS
TYPE>> Normal/Flying	TYPE>> Water/Flying	TYPE>> Water/Flying	TYPE>> Psychic
ABILITY>> Guts	ABILITY>> Keen Eye	ABILITY>> Keen Eye	ABILITY>> Synchronize/Trace

281 KIRLIA	282 GARDEVOIR	283 SURSKIT	284 MASQUERAIN
TYPE>> Psychic	TYPE>> Psychic	TYPE>> Bug/Water	TYPE>> Bug/Flying
ABILITY>> Synchronize/Trace	ABILITY>> Synchronize/Trace	ABILITY>> Swift Swim	ABILITY>> Intimidate

285 SHROOMISH	286 BRELOOM	287 SLAKOTH	288 VIGOROTH
TYPE>> Grass	TYPE>> Grass/Fighting	TYPE>> Normal	TYPE>> Normal
ABILITY>> Effect Spore	ABILITY>> Effect Spore	ABILITY>> Truant	ABILITY>> Vital Spirit

Ash and his friends were passing through a massive forest on their journey towards the Battle Pyramid.

"It seems like this forest goes on *forever*!" said May.

"Yeah, it's a big one all right!" Max agreed.

"Well, we'll be through soon enough!" said Brock. "Then we'll be near the Fennel Valley ruins."

"Sounds good!" cheered Ash. "We're ready to *rock*!"

At last they reached the edge of the forest.

"Yay! We made it!" May smiled.

"Wow, I hadn't seen the sun in such a long time, I'd forgotten what it looks like!" Max joked.

"Looks like a *great* time for a rest!" said Brock.

"You bet!" Max sighed.

DULES OF THE JUNGLE

Pikachu ran off to play with Aipom. But Aipom got lost in some long grass.
Suddenly a Weavile appeared in front of Aipom. Then it attacked!
Ash saw the puff of smoke from the explosion.
"What was that?" he cried.
"Beats *me*!" said Max.
Just then, Pikachu reappeared – without Aipom!

"Where's Aipom?" Ash asked. He ran to try to find his Pokémon, and stopped when he saw the Weavile. May checked her Pokédex.
"Weavile, The Sharp Claw Pokémon," said the Pokédex. "Weavile is the evolved form of Sneasel. It is extremely intelligent, and its sharp eyes see everything."

63

"You wanna battle, huh?" Ash asked.

The stray Weavile threw a shadowball at them. They only just dodged in time!

"I've had just about *enough*!" Ash yelled. "Pikachu! Use Thunderbolt!"

Pikachu attacked, but the stray Weavile dodged it at top speed.

"What a *dodge*!" Ash gasped, impressed.

Suddenly the Weavile hurled a massive shadowball at Pikachu!

"Dodge, Pikachu!" Ash shouted.
But it was too late – Pikachu was flung to Ash's feet!
Next, Aipom attacked the Weavile using Swift, but it wasn't fast enough!
"Weavile dodged it!" May gasped.
"Yeah – and at the speed of *lightning*!" said Brock.

"Use Double Team *now*!" Ash cried. Aipom attacked again, but the stray Weavile was far quicker. Aipom was hurt!

The friends rushed to Aipom's side.

"That was so *rough*!" said May, really worried.

"Weavile's gone!" said Max suddenly.

"What was *that* all about?" asked Brock in confusion.

"I saw the whole thing!" called a voice. A man was running towards them.

"Excuse me," said Ash. "Who are *you*?"

"We'll save that for later!" said the man. "Right *now* we've got to get this Aipom some *help*. I've got a little hut in the woods. Let's go!"

Ash and his friends followed the man.

Not far away, Team Rocket had also seen the whole thing.

"Amazing," said Jessie. "See *that*?"

"That Weavile wiped the *walls* with Aipom!" said James.

"My advice is to stay away from 'dat crazy kook at all *costs*!" said Meowth.

"Oh what do *you* know?" Jessie snapped. "Think of that lean jaw ... those deep-set eyes ... that no-nonsense take-no-prisoners attitude. Puh-leeze! Weavile's a *dreamboat*!"

"Grabbin' an' givin' to 'da Boss is good 'tinkin'!" said Meowth.

"Not *quite*," said Jessie. "We're going to grab it and give it to *yours truly*! This is love at *first sight*!"

Back at his hut, the man introduced himself as Kerrigan. He explained that he was in the Wilderness Guard Corps.

"It's *my* responsibility to watch this forest," he said.

Thanks a lot for helpin' us out like this!" said Ash.

"I'm sure glad everybody's safe!" said Kerrigan gently. "Aipom's going to be just *fine* after a good sleep."

"What's with that Weavile?" asked Brock.

"That Weavile's a stray," Kerrigan explained. "You see, there's a large group of Weavile and Sneasel, and they all live together here in the forest. But at some point that *particular* Weavile left the group, and started living out on its own."

The friends listened in amazement. "Whenever it sees people with Pokémon, it has to challenge them!" said Kerrigan. "But I'm afraid I haven't *any* idea what the motive is behind Weavile's actions." "There's *gotta* be a reason," said Brock.

"Right," Kerrigan agreed, standing up. "I think I'd better go and have a look around the area where this has all been taking *place*!"

"Kerrigan, *wait*!" said Ash. "I wanna go with you!"

The others wanted to go along too. "I *can't* let *other* Pokémon get beaten up the way that my Aipom did!" said Ash with passion.

Kerrigan led Ash and his friends
for what felt like miles.
"I don't see *anythin'* around here,"
said Ash.
"Pikachu, think you can smell if
Weavile's been hangin' around?"
Max asked.
Pikachu tried – and then seemed
to find something!

Meanwhile, Meowth had dressed
up as a Weavile and tried to make
friends with the stray Weavile.
But the real Weavile saw through
the disguise with its sharp eyes!
Meowth rushed back to Jessie
and James.
"'Dat dude told me if I eva'
trespassed on his toif again 'dere
was a Shadowball wit' *my* name
on it!" panicked Meowth.
"Give me a *break!*" screamed
Jessie in fury. "Get back *in* there!"
"Are you *nuts?*" Meowth panicked.
"I'll get used for *target practice!*"

Just then they heard a shout.
"It's Weavile!" cried Ash. "Over there!"
Team Rocket hid as Pikachu led Ash and his friends towards them. Pikachu started to speak to Weavile.
"Know what they're sayin'?" asked Max.
"Nah," said Ash.
"*You* do!" hissed Jessie to Meowth. "Translate or *else*!"
"Okay," said Meowth. "Foist Pikachu said 'Why are ya doin' that stuff?'. *Weavile* says, 'I don't have to answer to a little piece of yellow junk like *you*!'"
"And *then*?" asked James.
"'Den *zip*!" said Meowth. 'Dose two were speakin' faster 'dan a *freight train*!"
"You are a *sorry* excuse for a Pokémon!" screamed Jessie, forgetting that they were hiding!

"*You* guys?" yelled Ash furiously. "Weavile, sir," said Jessie. "You're a hunk! Let's you and I fly *away*! Weavile and I, up in the sky!"

"Man, she's *weird*!" said Max. "We're not gonna let you do that when we've got *battlin'* to do!" said Ash.

"Battle *yourself*!" Jessie yelled. "No one puts a mark on my Weaviley-poo's face!"

Suddenly, there was a rustling in the hedge. Then a Sneasel appeared and started to speak to Weavile.

"*You* start translating or *I* use you for a *bullseye*!" Jessie snapped at Meowth.

"Foist Weavile says, 'Why'd ya follow me?'" Meowth said. "An' 'den she says, 'I'm not followin'! I'm *escapin'*!'"

"Escapin' from *what*?" Ash wondered.

"'Dat Sneasel babe's sayin' it wasn't too long ago 'dat all 'da Weavile an' Sneasel used to live peacefully in 'da forest," said Meowth. "Until 'dis rogue Weavile suddenly appears outta *nowhere*, ready to stir it up!"

Meowth explained that the stray Weavile had once been the leader of the tribe, but a rogue Weavile had challenged it for leadership. The rogue Weavile had won, so the old leader had turned into a stray!

"Weavile had one goal – to get big an' strong!" Meowth translated. "But 'dat rogue Weavile toined out to be a real bad egg. A real nasty an' mean Pokémon! Finally, 'dis Sneasel got sick an' tired of bein' kicked around an' high-tailed it on outta 'dere!"

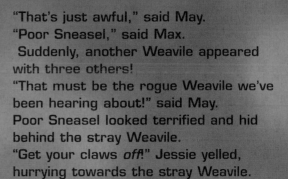

"That's just awful," said May.
"Poor Sneasel," said Max.
Suddenly, another Weavile appeared with three others!
"That must be the rogue Weavile we've been hearing about!" said May.
Poor Sneasel looked terrified and hid behind the stray Weavile.
"Get your claws *off*!" Jessie yelled, hurrying towards the stray Weavile.

"Wait!" called Meowth. "Jessie!"
"Stop!" yelled James.
But Jessie wasn't listening.
"Come with *me*, Weavil*ee*, for an evil as old as the *galaxy*!" she said in her sweetest voice.
But the Weavile fired a Shadowball at her.
Team Rocket blasted off again!

"That Weavile wants Sneasel back!" said Max, looking at the rogue Weavile.

"Whadda we *do*?" cried Max. Suddenly Ash had an idea! He turned to the stray Weavile. "You *like* that?" he taunted. "You like that they're gonna drag your Sneasel friend back with 'em? Are you just gonna stand there and let 'em *do* that? You let that Weavile walk all over you *before*! An' now – you're just gonna let Weavile walk all over you *again*?" The stray Weavile turned to look at Ash, then turned back to face the other Weavile.

The rogue Weavile ordered its servants to surround Sneasel and the stray Weavile. "Now Pikachu, use Thunderbolt!" Ash yelled. Pikachu defeated the servant Weaviles easily! "C'mon!" Ash cried to the stray Weavile. "I thought you said you were gonna get so *strong*!"

The rogue Weavile and the stray Weavile faced each other again. The new leader and the old one! "Looks like this is the deciding *battle*!" said Kerrigan.
The rogue Weavile fired a Shadowball – but so did the stray Weavile! They dodged each other's attacks.
"Whoa!" cried Max in amazement.
"Weavile!" yelled Ash.
"No *way*!" Max shouted.

"Now we'll see the result of *all* that trainin'!"
said Ash.
The stray Weavile fired another Shadowball at
its opponent.
Weavile leapt into the air. It was a tremendous
battle! They dodged and fought as fast as lightning.
"Look *out*!" Ash yelled.
The stray grabbed the rogue's hand and threw him.
When the rogue hit the ground, the stray climbed
on top of him. He had won!

"All that trainin' sure paid *off*!" said Ash.
Sneasel persuaded the stray Weavile to
make a truce with the rogue Weavile.
"Excellent!" said Brock. "It looks like
everyone's accepting the way things are!"
"Great!" said Kerrigan. "Perhaps now
they can live in peace, and this forest can
begin getting back to the way things
used to be!"

Back at Kerrigan's hut, Aipom was much better and the friends got ready to leave.
"Thanks for lettin' us come along with you, Kerrigan!" said Ash.
"My pleasure!" Kerrigan smiled. "Good luck at your next battle, Ash!"
"Hey thanks!" said Ash. "Can't wait for the Battle Pyramid!"

289 SLAKING	290 NINCADA	291 NINJASK	292 SHEDINJA
TYPE>> Normal	TYPE>> Bug/Ground	TYPE>> Bug/Flying	TYPE>> Bug/Ghost
ABILITY>> Truant	ABILITY>> Compoundeyes	ABILITY>> Speed Boost	ABILITY>> Wonder Guard

293 WHISMUR	294 LOUDRED	295 EXPLOUD	296 MAKUHITA
TYPE>> Normal	TYPE>> Normal	TYPE>> Normal	TYPE>> Fighting
ABILITY>> Soundproof	ABILITY>> Soundproof	ABILITY>> Soundproof	ABILITY>> Thick Fat/Guts

297 HARIYAMA	298 AZURILL	299 NOSEPASS	300 SKITTY
TYPE>> Fighting	TYPE>> Normal	TYPE>> Rock	TYPE>> Normal
ABILITY>> Thick Fat/Guts	ABILITY>> Thick Fat/Huge Power	ABILITY>> Sturdy/Magnet Pull	ABILITY>> Cute Charm

301 DELCATTY	302 SABLEYE	303 MAWILE	304 ARON
TYPE>> Normal	TYPE>> Dark/Ghost	TYPE>> Steel	TYPE>> Steel/Rock
ABILITY>> Cute Charm	ABILITY>> Keen Eye	ABILITY>> Hyper Cutter/Intimidate	ABILITY>> Sturdy/Rock Head

305 LAIRON	306 AGGRON	307 MEDITITE	308 MEDICHAM
TYPE>> Steel/Rock	TYPE>> Steel/Rock	TYPE>> Fighting/Psychic	TYPE>> Fighting/Psychic
ABILITY>> Sturdy/Rock Head	ABILITY>> Sturdy/Rock Head	ABILITY>> Pure Power	ABILITY>> Pure Power

309 ELECTRIKE	310 MANECTRIC	311 PLUSLE	312 MINUN
TYPE>> Electric	TYPE>> Electric	TYPE>> Electric	TYPE>> Electric
ABILITY>> Static/Lightningrod	ABILITY>> Static/Lightningrod	ABILITY>> Plus	ABILITY>> Minus

313 VOLBEAT	314 ILLUMISE	315 ROSELIA	316 GULPIN
TYPE>> Bug	TYPE>> Bug	TYPE>> Grass/Poison	TYPE>> Poison
ABILITY>> Illuminate/Swarm	ABILITY>> Oblivious	ABILITY>> Natural Cure/Poison Point	ABILITY>> Liquid Ooze/Sticky Hold
317 SWALOT	318 CARVANHA	319 SHARPEDO	320 WAILMER
TYPE>> Poison	TYPE>> Water/Dark	TYPE>> Water/Dark	TYPE>> Water
ABILITY>> Liquid Ooze/Sticky Hold	ABILITY>> Rough Skin	ABILITY>> Rough Skin	ABILITY>> Water Veil/Oblivious
321 WAILORD	322 NUMEL	323 CAMERUPT	324 TORKOAL
TYPE>> Water	TYPE>> Fire/Ground	TYPE>> Fire/Ground	TYPE>> Fire
ABILITY>> Water Veil/Oblivious	ABILITY>> Oblivious	ABILITY>> Magma Armour	ABILITY>> White Smoke
325 SPOINK	326 GRUMPIG	327 SPINDA	328 TRAPINCH
TYPE>> Psychic	TYPE>> Psychic	TYPE>> Normal	TYPE>> Ground
ABILITY>> Thick Fat/Own Tempo	ABILITY>> Thick Fat/Own Tempo	ABILITY>> Own Tempo	ABILITY>> Hyper Cutter/Arena Trap
329 VIBRAVA	330 FLYGON	331 CACNEA	332 CACTURNE
TYPE>> Ground/Dragon	TYPE>> Ground/Dragon	TYPE>> Grass	TYPE>> Grass/Dark
ABILITY>> Levitate	ABILITY>> Levitate	ABILITY>> Sand Veil	ABILITY>> Sand Veil
333 SWABLU	334 ALTARIA	335 ZANGOOSE	336 SEVIPER
TYPE>> Normal/Flying	TYPE>> Dragon/Flying	TYPE>> Normal	TYPE>> Poison
ABILITY>> Natural Cure	ABILITY>> Natural Cure	ABILITY>> Immunity	ABILITY>> Shed Skin

337 LUNATONE
TYPE>> Rock/Psychic
ABILITY>> Levitate

338 SOLROCK
TYPE>> Rock/Psychic
ABILITY>> Levitate

339 BARBOACH
TYPE>> Water/Ground
ABILITY>> Oblivious

340 WHISCASH
TYPE>> Water/Ground
ABILITY>> Oblivious

341 CORPHISH
TYPE>> Water
ABILITY>> Hyper Cutter/Shell Armour

342 CRAWDAUNT
TYPE>> Water/Dark
ABILITY>> Hyper Cutter/Shell Armour

343 BALTOY
TYPE>> Ground/Psychic
ABILITY>> Levitate

344 CLAYDOL
TYPE>> Ground/Psychic
ABILITY>> Levitate

345 LILEEP
TYPE>> Rock/Grass
ABILITY>> Suction Cups

346 CRADILY
TYPE>> Rock/Grass
ABILITY>> Suction Cups

347 ANORITH
TYPE>> Rock/Bug
ABILITY>> Battle Armour

348 ARMALDO
TYPE>> Rock/Bug
ABILITY>> Battle Armour

349 FEEBAS
TYPE>> Water
ABILITY>> Swift Swim

350 MILOTIC
TYPE>> Water
ABILITY>> Marvel Scale

351 CASTFORM
TYPE>> Normal
ABILITY>> Forecast

352 KECLEON
TYPE>> Normal
ABILITY>> Colour Change

353 SHUPPET
TYPE>> Ghost
ABILITY>> Insomnia

354 BANETTE
TYPE>> Ghost
ABILITY>> Insomnia

355 DUSKULL
TYPE>> Ghost
ABILITY>> Levitate

356 DUSCLOPS
TYPE>> Ghost
ABILITY>> Pressure

357 TROPIUS
TYPE>> Grass/Flying
ABILITY>> Chlorophyll

358 CHIMECHO
TYPE>> Psychic
ABILITY>> Levitate

359 ABSOL
TYPE>> Dark
ABILITY>> Pressure

360 WYNAUT
TYPE>> Psychic
ABILITY>> Shadow Tag

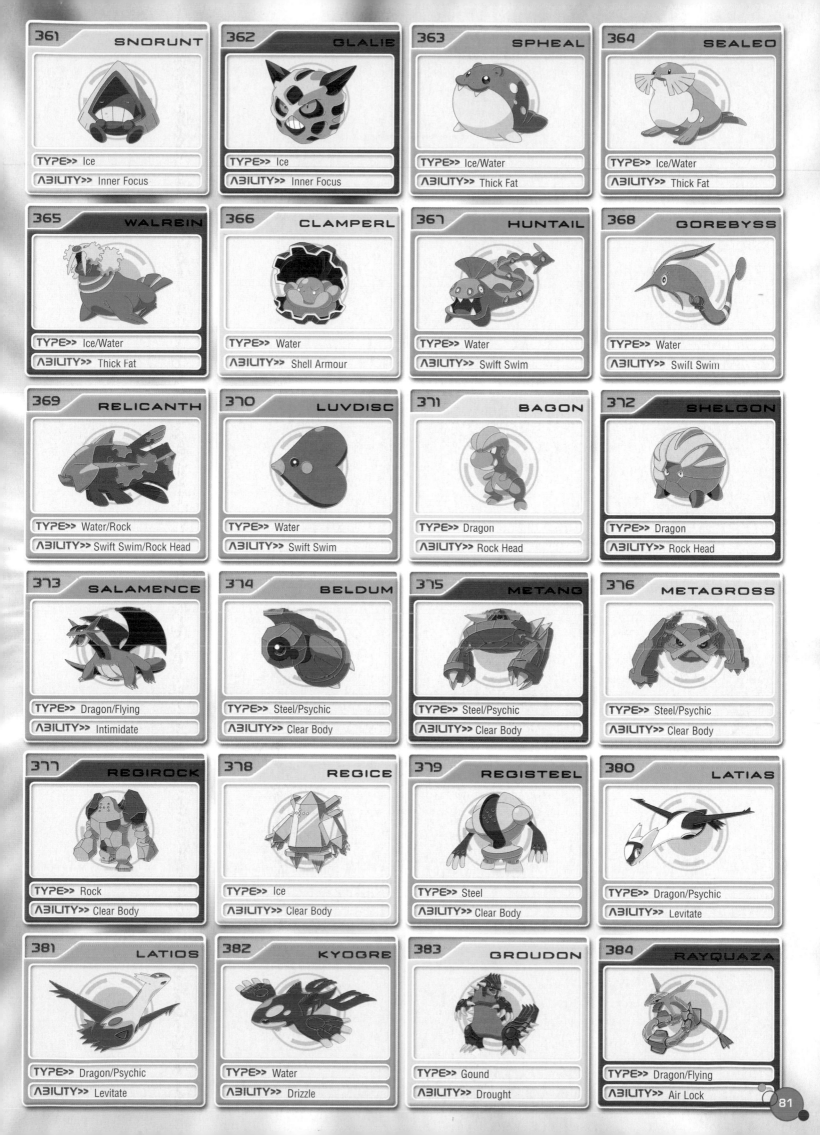

361 SNORUNT	362 GLALIE	363 SPHEAL	364 SEALEO
TYPE>> Ice	TYPE>> Ice	TYPE>> Ice/Water	TYPE>> Ice/Water
ABILITY>> Inner Focus	ABILITY>> Inner Focus	ABILITY>> Thick Fat	ABILITY>> Thick Fat

365 WALREIN	366 CLAMPERL	367 HUNTAIL	368 GOREBYSS
TYPE>> Ice/Water	TYPE>> Water	TYPE>> Water	TYPE>> Water
ABILITY>> Thick Fat	ABILITY>> Shell Armour	ABILITY>> Swift Swim	ABILITY>> Swift Swim

369 RELICANTH	370 LUVDISC	371 BAGON	372 SHELGON
TYPE>> Water/Rock	TYPE>> Water	TYPE>> Dragon	TYPE>> Dragon
ABILITY>> Swift Swim/Rock Head	ABILITY>> Swift Swim	ABILITY>> Rock Head	ABILITY>> Rock Head

373 SALAMENCE	374 BELDUM	375 METANG	376 METAGROSS
TYPE>> Dragon/Flying	TYPE>> Steel/Psychic	TYPE>> Steel/Psychic	TYPE>> Steel/Psychic
ABILITY>> Intimidate	ABILITY>> Clear Body	ABILITY>> Clear Body	ABILITY>> Clear Body

377 REGIROCK	378 REGICE	379 REGISTEEL	380 LATIAS
TYPE>> Rock	TYPE>> Ice	TYPE>> Steel	TYPE>> Dragon/Psychic
ABILITY>> Clear Body	ABILITY>> Clear Body	ABILITY>> Clear Body	ABILITY>> Levitate

381 LATIOS	382 KYOGRE	383 GROUDON	384 RAYQUAZA
TYPE>> Dragon/Psychic	TYPE>> Water	TYPE>> Gound	TYPE>> Dragon/Flying
ABILITY>> Levitate	ABILITY>> Drizzle	ABILITY>> Drought	ABILITY>> Air Lock

A sh and May had reached the second round Battle at the Terracotta Pokémon Contest. The massive auditorium was filled with people! Attacks rocketed back and forth at breakneck speed! But time ran out *just* as their Blaziken and Sceptile were in the midst of their strongest moves. After an *overwhelming* battle explosion, one important question remained. *Who won*?

HOME IS WHERE THE START IS!

Time's up, but who is our *winner*?" boomed the announcer. "The judges have determined that both remaining point scores are *even*! Nurse Joy?"
"In the event of a tie, according to Contest rules, both Ash and May are declared the winners!" Nurse Joy declared.
"What an awesome way to end a great Contest!" cried Max.
"Right!" said Brock.
"Great battle, May," said Ash.
"Thanks Ash, same to you!" said May. Sceptile and Blaziken congratulated each other too!

A fitting end to a *great* Terracotta Pokémon Contest!" said the announcer. "And now Nurse Joy will present both of our winners with the Terracotta medal!"
There was only one medal, but May and Ash knew how to settle this!
"Okay Sceptile, Leaf Blade!" Ash cried. Sceptile used its attack to cut the medal in half? "All right!" said Ash. "We got ourselves the Terracotta Medal!"
"Now that looks like a *real* friendship!" said the announcer. "Sharing their victory, and sharing their *medal* as well!"

After the ceremony, the friends prepared to tuck in to a celebration meal. "Hold on, guys!" said May. "There's something I need to tell you first."

"What's on your mind?" asked Ash.

"I've decided to go and enter the Johto Pokémon Contests *by myself*!" May said with a gulp.

"But what about Max?" asked Brock.

"Max, I know if you came along with me I'd start to depend on you," said May. "You remember when we all first met up? I hadn't the slightest what I wanted for myself. But now – well, things are different."

May's friends were listening carefully. "After travelling around with you all, I know *exactly* what I want to do!" she continued. "There's a lot more for me to learn – lots more Contests for me to be in, new ways of presenting my Pokémon – *lots* of ways to make them *shine!*"

"You're right, May," said Brock.

"Sounds good to me!" said Ash.

Max walked away and Ash went to speak to him.

"I know it's hard knowin' you won't be goin' too," said Ash.

"Lately I've started feelin' *jealous* of May," said Max sadly. "See, when you and May were battlin' back there, I've never *seen* her so psyched! But all I could do was watch, and it made me wish I could grow up quick so *I* could do that too."

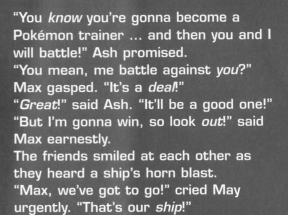

"You *know* you're gonna become a Pokémon trainer ... and then you and I will battle!" Ash promised.
"You mean, me battle against *you*?" Max gasped. "It's a *deal*!"
"*Great*!" said Ash. "It'll be a good one!"
"But I'm gonna win, so look *out*!" said Max earnestly.
The friends smiled at each other as they heard a ship's horn blast.
"Max, we've got to go!" cried May urgently. "That's our *ship*!"

Soon Max and May were waving goodbye from the deck of the ship.
"Bye, you guys!" called Brock and Ash.
With a final wave, they sailed into the sunset.

Brock and Ash walked on until they reached a crossroads.

"Pallet Town's to the left," said Ash.

"Pewter City's to the right," said Brock.

"So, then ..." said Ash quietly.

"Yeah," said Brock.

"This is it," said Ash, as his stomach rumbled. "Whoa, I'm so *hungry*!"

"Pallet Town is really close by, and they're going to have a big feast for you, aren't they?" Brock grinned.

"I *did* tell Mum I was comin' back today!" said Ash, suddenly excited. "Man, I hope she's got enough *food*!"

"I guess some things never change," laughed Brock. "All right, I'm outta here!"

The two friends went their separate ways.

Team Rocket were floating above in their balloon.

"So they went and broke up that old Twerp gang, eh?" said Jessie, fascinated. "A *solo* Twerp makes for an easy *catch*! Now, about that *Pikachu* ... do you see anything?"

"Not even 'da tiniest yellow-bellied Twoipish blob!" said Meowth, looking through his binoculars.

"When it comes to catching Pikachu we're batting *zip*!" said James.

"Every time I get my paws on 'dat Pika-pain, it pries itself right out!" said Meowth. "We should quit while we're behind!"

"Are you saying we should throw in the Team Rocket *towel*?" said Jessie, shocked. "Have you forgotten we exist to catch *Pikachu*?"

Suddenly, there was an electrical surge
of light below them. They peered over
the edge of the balloon.
"Thunderbolt, perhaps?" asked Jessie.
"Pika-power!" said James, excited.
But when they looked through their
binoculars, they saw an unknown
Pokémon!
"I've seen lotsa Pokémon, but 'dat's a
new one on me," said Meowth.
"Let's catch it!" said Jessie.

Electivire was munching an apple as
Team Rocket crept up on it.
"*Lunch* time means it's *crunch* time,"
said Jessie.
"Then crunch ... but *gently*," said James.
"You mean like 'dis?" shouted Meowth,
catching the Pokémon in his net.
"You're *through* with lunch!" cried
Team Rocket.

Nearby, Ash saw Electivire's frantic bolts of electricity shooting above the trees.
"Pikachu, see *that*?" Ash gasped.
"We'd better check it out!"

Electivire was struggling in the net when a stranger yelled at Team Rocket.
"Hey!" he bellowed. "Whadda you three think you're doin' to my Pokémon?"
"Playing?" said James feebly.
At that moment, Ash appeared.
"Team Rocket!" he cried. "I'm gettin' tired of all this bad stuff you do! Well you're gonna have to battle *us*!"

"Don't sweat it, Ash!" said the stranger.

Ash and Pikachu saw him and gasped.

"Long time no see, Ashie Boy!" he continued.

"It's Gary!" cried Ash.

"Don't worry, Electivire," Gary told his Pokémon. "There are *other* ways to win even if your Electric attacks don't work! Iron Tail, let's *go*!"

Electivire used its attack to burst out of the net. Then it used Thunderpunch to defeat Team Rocket

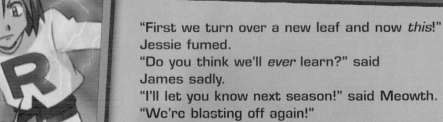

"First we turn over a new leaf and now *this*!" Jessie fumed.

"Do you think we'll *ever* learn?" said James sadly.

"I'll let you know next season!" said Meowth. "We're blasting off again!"

Ash tried to look Electivire up on his Pokédex, but there was no data!

"I got Electivire in Sinnoh," said Gary. "Pretty cool, don't you think?"

"Sure!" said Ash in excitement. "I'll bet Sinnoh's got *lots* of awesome Pokémon! Hey Gary, wanna have a *battle*?"

"No thanks," said Gary. "Electivire used up too much energy for any more. But if you really wanna battle I'll be in Grandpa's lab, so come back later!"

When Ash arrived home, his mother wasn't there.

"Maybe she went shoppin' or somethin'," Ash said. "Whaddaya say we go over and say hi to Professor Oak?"

Soon Ash was walking into Professor Oak's lab ... but no one was there either.

"Professor Oak! Tracey!" he called. "Hey, where *is* everybody? This is so *weird*. I told 'em we were comin' home."

Suddenly there was a shout of welcome. It was a surprise party!
"Welcome home dear!" said Delia Ketchum, Ash's mother.
"Hi Mum," said Ash happily. "What a *surprise*!"
Ash proudly showed his mother the plaque he had been given for winning the Battle Frontier.
"We just wanted to give you a *proper* welcome home!" said Professor Oak.
"So come on!" said Tracey. "Let's get this party *started*!"

"There's one thing I need to do *first*, if you don't mind," Ash said.
"Go right ahead!" said Professor Oak.
"Hey Gary, your Electivire back up to speed?" Ash asked with a twinkle in his eye.
"Yeah!" said Gary. "Ready anytime *you* are!"
"Great! 'cause that's *now*!" said Ash.

The Pokémon battle between Ash and Pikachu and Gary and Electivire began!
"Pikachu! Let's use Thunderbolt!" Ash said.
"Electivire, Thunderbolt!" cried Gary.
The two Thunderbolts clashed!
"*Well*, those Thunderbolts are evenly matched!" said Professor Oak.
"Let's win this!" said Ash to Pikachu. "Now, Quick Attack!"
"Dodge!" yelled Gary.
Electivire leapt high into the air.

"It *flies*?" gasped Ash.
"Iron Tail!" cried Gary.
"Use Iron Tail as well!" Ash exclaimed.
Pikachu and Electivire clashed evenly again.
"Whoa, that Electivire's powerful all right!" said Ash. "But hey, we can't *lose* – we won the *Battle Frontier*!"

"Up in the air Electivire's *defenceless*!" said Ash. "Pikachu! Volt Tackle!"
"Come on, Ash!" said Gary smugly. "Electivire! Protect!"
Pikachu was stunned by Electivire's protective force field!
"Now, use Thunderpunch, *go*!" Gary shouted.
The Thunderpunch sent Pikachu flying backwards. He crashed to the ground!
"Pikachu!" Ash called.
"Pikachu can't battle!" Tracey declared. "Electivire's the winner! And the victor is Gary!"
"Electivire, great job," Gary said.
"Pikachu, I'm so sorry," Ash said. "I really thought we could win it!"
"Hey Ash," said Gary. "It's great that you won the Battle Frontier, but that doesn't mean you can relax! There are all sorts of tough Pokémon in Sinnoh that you don't even *know* about yet! The world is a *big* place."

After Gary left, Ash thought about what he had said.
"Tough Pokémon, huh? The world's a big *place*, huh? I know *just* what I'm gonna do!" His mother looked at him, startled.
"I'm gonna head over to Sinnoh!" said Ash.

Next day, Ash was ready to set out on his new adventure. Professor Oak promised to take care of his other Pokémon.
"Now, when you get to the Sinnoh region, I want you to head over to Sandgem Town and look up Professor Rowan," said the Professor. "Brilliant, an expert on Pokémon evolution and an old friend and colleague of mine!"
"I'll do it!" said Ash.

"And now, I'd like to present you with this little present," said Professor Oak. "It contains *everything* you need to know about the Sinnoh region!"
It was a brand-new Pokédex!
"Professor, thank you!" gasped Ash in excitement
"My pleasure!" said Professor Oak. "Good luck, Ash!"

Soon Ash and Pikachu were on a ship to the Sinnoh region.
"The Sinnoh region," sighed Ash to Pikachu happily. "You *ready*, buddy?"
Suddenly, the wind blew his hat off. It was caught by ... Aipom!
"Hey Aipom!" Ash cried. "You followed us all this *way*?"
Aipom didn't want to be left behind!
"Welcome aboard!" laughed Ash.
"Awesome! All right, Sinnoh Island, look *out*! You'd better get ready for *us*!"

Ash and friends have returned to the Kanto region. On their travels they have many adventures and encounter their most intense challenge yet - the Battle Frontier! Ash confronts the Frontier Brains and battles his way through this circuit of seven elite trainers.

You will need:

- A marker for each player
- A dice.

1. Draw Pokémon cards to decide who goes first. The player with the most powerful attacks starts the game.
2. Throw the dice and move your marker along the squares.
3. Check out the instructions on the square where you land and do what they say!
4. The first player to reach the Battle Pyramid is the winner!

Oh no! You are attacked by the Pike Queen before you reach the Battle Pike. **GO BACK TO SQUARE 1.**

Congratulations! You made it to the Battle Factory. **HAVE ANOTHER GO!**

You put on a great show against Tucker at the Battle Dome! **HAVE ANOTHER GO.**

Well done! You have defeated Greta at the Battle Arena. **GO FORWARD TWO SPACES.**

BATTLE BOARDGAME

A game for 2 or more players.

Join the race to complete the Battle Frontier contests! Follow the instructions and work your way around the game. You can have as many players as you like. Good luck!

29

30

31

32

33

34

35

37

38

39

40

You stop at the Battle Palace to meditate with Spenser. **MISS A GO.**

41

43

42

Anabel's Psychic-type Pokémon defeats you at the Battle Tower. **GO BACK THREE SPACES.**

49

48

47

46

45

50

51

52

53

You stop to confront Brandon at the Battle Pyramid. **MISS A GO.**

54

CONGRATULATIONS
You are the first to complete the Battle Frontier contests!

POKÉMON

TM

BATTLE FRONTIER

Ash and friends have returned to the Kanto region. On their travels they have many adventures and encounter their most intense challenge yet - the Battle Frontier! Ash confronts the Frontier Brains and battles his way through this circuit of seven elite trainers. Both Ash and May have new Pokémon on their side, but May encounters old rivals and friends when she enters Kanto's Pokémon Contests.

NOLAND

Noland is a mechanical whiz and Factory Head of the Battle Factory. Not only that, but he's even managed to befriend a Legendary Pokémon, Articuno!

GRETA

Arena Tycoon Greta is a martial arts master, so it's no surprise that challengers at her Battle Arena will face formidable Fighting -type Pokémon.

TUCKER

Tucker is the star of the Battle Dome, where cheering fans come to watch spectacular battles! As Dome Ace, he combines showmanship with the skills of a top strategist.

LUCY

Battle Pike challengers will find themselves up against Lucy, the cool, composed Pike Queen. For Lucy, a strong offense is the best – and only – defense!

SPENSER

Palace Maven Spenser is the kindly Frontier Brain in charge of the Battle Palace. With his love for nature, it's no wonder that his battleground is as big as the outdoors!

ANABEL

Anabel, the Battle Tower's petite Salon Maiden, has a gentle way with Pokémon. But when it comes to battle, her Psychic-type Pokémon can hit hard and fast!

BRANDON

The Pyramid King Brandon lives in the Battle Pyramid, which can become airborne by the use of turbines. He uses trios of Legendary Pokémon, but watch out - he doesn't like to be disagreed with

NEW FACES!

Brock is sharing a joke with this friendly Bonsly!
Come and meet some of the new Pokémon that
he and his friends have discovered...

NAME :: MANAPHY

TYPE :: WATER

WEIGHT :: 1.4KG

HEIGHT :: 0.3M

CHARACTERISTICS ::

Manaphy is a Legendary Pokémon, often referred to as the 'Prince of the Sea' due to its revered status among sea Pokémon. Its skin feels like silicon to touch and 80% of its body is water. Manaphy is slightly cold to touch because its body temperature is slightly cooler than that of humans. Manaphy can happily survive in either fresh or salt water.

NAME :: LUCARIO

TYPE :: STEEL + FIGHTING

WEIGHT :: 54.0KG

HEIGHT :: 1.2M

CHARACTERISTICS ::

Lucario is perfect for either defence or attack. It can keenly sense Aura - which is an energy emitted by all things - being able to both see it and control it. The four tassles on its head are very sensitive. They fan out when they detect Aura.

NAME :: WEAVILE

TYPE :: DARK + ICE

WEIGHT :: 34.0KG

HEIGHT :: 1.1M

CHARACTERISTICS ::

Weavile operate in small packs of 2-6 members. Using their sharp claws, they carve plant and feather designs into blocks of ice. Some people think that these designs are territory markers and signals to their pack members. Some believe that the designs form part of a ceremony.

NAME :: MIME JR.

TYPE :: PSYCHIC

WEIGHT :: 13.0KG

HEIGHT :: 0.6M

CHARACTERISTICS ::

Mime Jr. can mimic the movement of anything it sees. If stared at, it will constantly change its expression, perhaps by screwing up its mouth or puffing out its cheeks. It can detect fluctuations in its opponent's emotional state. If it senses danger, it will create a barrier and flee.

NAME :: BUIZEL

TYPE :: WATER

WEIGHT :: 29.5KG

HEIGHT :: 0.7M

CHARACTERISTICS ::

Buizel have round collar-rings and two-pronged tails. The collar-ring can inflate, allowing Buizel to stay afloat in the water with just their faces peeking above the water's surface. They move through the water by twirling their tails at incredible speeds and using them as a propeller. Despite these adaptations to aquatic life, they spend most of their time on land.

NAME :: MUNCHLAX

TYPE :: NORMAL

WEIGHT :: 105.0KG

HEIGHT :: 0.6KG

CHARACTERISTICS ::

Each day at exactly the same time, Munchlax take their sole daily meal in one large portion. When this daily mealtime is approaching, Munchlax become very restless, with their bellies growling loudly. They carry large amounts of food hidden in their fur. This food sometimes spills out when the Munchlax is knocked or trips over.

NAME :: BONSLY

TYPE :: ROCK

WEIGHT :: 15KG

HEIGHT :: 0.5M

CHARACTERISTICS ::

Bonsly looks like a Grass-type, but is actually a Rock-type. They look just like a Bonsai tree! Bonsly are often called cry-babies because they seem to be weeping most of the time. However, these are not tears. Bonsly have to control their body fluid levels as they become weak if they are too high! They keep their fluid levels under control by letting out water from glands near their eyes.

NAME :: MANTYKE

TYPE :: WATER + FLYING

WEIGHT :: 65.0KG

HEIGHT :: 1M

CHARACTERISTICS ::

Mantyke gracefully glide through the ocean, and they can sometimes be seen jumping into to the air as high as 10 metres. Mantyke are very intelligent and they like humans. They prefer to swim in schools, leaving trails of bubbles behind their side fins as they cut through the water.

NAME :: CHATOT

TYPE :: NORMAL + FLYING

WEIGHT :: 1.9KG

HEIGHT :: 0.5M

CHARACTERISTICS ::

Chatot are instantly recognisable by their heads, which are shaped like musical notes - and, if not by their heads, they will certainly be recognised by their ability to mimic human words. When they mimics human words, their tail feathers shake side to side like a metronome tapping out a beat. Their easy-going natures and lack of awareness can often lead them into dangerous situations.

WEAVILE:: C

LUCARIO:: E

These Pokémon have lost their shadows! Can you work out which shadow belongs to each of the Pokémon and help to reunite them?

ANSWERS

CROSSWORDS - PAGE 11

1. BULBASAUR
2. SHELLOSHELLOS (H E L L O L L)
3. PIKEQUEEN
4. NONOLAND (N O L O N D)
5. SPOINK
6. BATTLEPYRAMID
7. TEAMAROCKET
8. MEOWTH
9. WALREIN
PIKACHU (P I K A C H U)